Friend of the Everglades

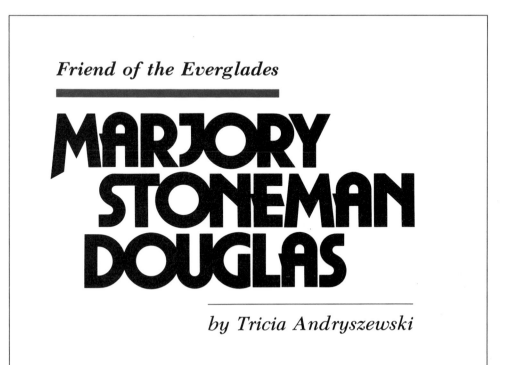

MARJORY STONEMAN DOUGLAS

by Tricia Andryszewski

A Gateway Green Biography
The Millbrook Press
Brookfield, Connecticut

Cover photograph courtesy of the Miami *Herald*
Cover background photograph courtesy of Everglades National
Park, National Park Service, U.S. Department of the Interior

Photographs courtesy of Wide World Photos: pp. 4, 35, 42;
Florida State Archives: pp. 7, 10, 22; Everglades National Park,
National Park Service, U.S. Department of the Interior: pp. 13,
14, 17, 21 (top: Mike Biaha, bottom: Williams), 25; U.S. Navy,
courtesy Harry S. Truman Library: p. 29 (top); Miami *Herald*:
pp. 29 (bottom), 38; The Orlando Sentinel: p. 32 (both).

Map by Frank Senyk

Library of Congress Cataloging-in-Publication Data
Andryszewski, Tricia, 1956–
Marjory Stoneman Douglas, friend of the Everglades / by
Tricia Andryszewski.
p. cm. — (A Gateway green biography)
Includes bibliographical references (p.) and index.
Summary: This book tells the story of the life and work of
Marjory Stoneman Douglas, an environmentalist who worked
to preserve the Florida Everglades for more than sixty years.
ISBN 1-56294-384-7 (lib. bdg.)
1. Douglas, Marjory Stoneman — Juvenile literature.
2. Conservationists — Florida — Biography — Juvenile literature.
3. Nature conservation — Florida — Everglades — Juvenile
literature. [1. Douglas, Marjory Stoneman. 2. Conservationists.
3. Everglades (Fla.)] I. Title. II. Series.
QH31.D645A84   1994
333.91'8'0975939092 — dc20   [B]   93-26731   CIP   AC

Published by The Millbrook Press
2 Old New Milford Road
Brookfield, Connecticut 06804

Marjory Stoneman Douglas

Marjory Stoneman Douglas at her hundredth birthday celebration. She worked to protect Florida's Everglades since the 1920s.

Under the hot Florida sun, in April 1990, 100-year-old Marjory Stoneman Douglas stood up in front of a crowd and said: "This is a very great day, because it proves to me what I've been believing all along — that more and more people are beginning to believe in the environment."

The crowd had gathered to celebrate the twentieth Earth Day and to celebrate Marjory Stoneman Douglas's hundredth birthday. Douglas was there to urge them to save the Everglades, the vast grassy wetlands that runs down the center of southern Florida. "It's got to be done for the future of Florida," she said. "If we don't keep the Everglades wet, [it will] be a desert, and no one will be able to live here."

Throughout her long life, Douglas saw great changes in the Everglades. Many of these changes were dangerous threats to the nature of the Everglades. She knew that *all* life in southern Florida — animals, plants, and people — needs a healthy Everglades, and she never got tired of urging people to save southern Florida's unique natural pattern of life.

Who was Marjory Stoneman Douglas, and how did she come to be the best friend of the Everglades?

She was born in Minneapolis, Minnesota, on April 7, 1890, and grew up far away from the Everglades. Marjory's parents separated when she was six years old, and Marjory and her mother went to live with Marjory's grandparents in Taunton, Massachusetts. Marjory's Aunt Fanny, her mother's sister, also shared this house with them. The house had a large attic with a spare room where Marjory sometimes went to "get away from grown-ups. Being an only child," she said, "I often felt there were too many grown-ups around for just me."

Marjory's childhood, a century ago, was very different from life in the United States today. Here's her description of summer evenings when she was a young girl:

We had three elm trees on our lot and all the way down the street there were elm trees. . . . Everyone had front porches. In the summer people would be sitting on their porches up and down the streets

*Marjory at age
one and a half.*

and the moonlight would be coming through the elm trees and the city fathers would very economically turn off the city lights. That was wonderful, people on porches enjoying the moonlight . . . and my mother and aunt would bring out the guitar and banjo and sing the kind of sentimental songs they sang in those days, always ending with "Good Night Ladies." All the people on the porches would applaud, and you had a lovely sense of a community enjoying an evening. It was so lovely in itself you could never forget it.

Marjory loved reading and was an intelligent student. Although it was very unusual for a young woman to attend college in those days, Marjory Stoneman graduated from Wellesley College in Massachusetts in 1912.

Some unhappy years followed. Marjory's mother died. Marjory worked at several dull jobs that didn't suit her. When she got married, to Kenneth Douglas, that worked out badly, too.

Marjory Stoneman Douglas left her whole early life behind in 1915, when she moved to Miami, Florida. When she first arrived there, she saw that

"Miami was no more than a glorified railroad terminal." Fewer than five thousand people lived there. The now-famous beach community had not yet been built. "Most of Miami Beach was a blank layer of sand with streets laid out — no houses, just markers," Douglas remembered.

Douglas's father, Frank Stoneman, ran the town's morning newspaper, the Miami *Herald*. Her first real career, as a writer, began when she went to work at this newspaper. But World War I soon interrupted. Douglas explained how:

I was supposed to do a story for the Herald *on the first woman to enlist [in the U.S. Naval Reserve] in the state of Florida. We'd been told that the wife of the plumber . . . across the street from the newspaper was going to sign up. I arrived at the ship and the next thing I knew I was sticking up my hand, swearing to protect and defend the United States of America from all enemies whatsoever. . . . I called my father at the newspaper and said, "Look, I got the story on the first woman to enlist. It turned out to be me." He said, "I admire your patriotism but it leaves us a little shorthanded."*

Miami was a small town when Douglas first went there in 1915, about the time this photo of a downtown street was taken. But it quickly grew into a big city and popular resort area.

After a year in the Naval Reserve, Douglas then joined the American Red Cross, which sent her to Paris, France. She worked for the Red Cross there and throughout Europe, writing news stories about Red Cross activities during the war. When the war ended, she helped with the huge job of resettling people who had lost their homes during the fighting.

When Douglas returned to Miami in 1920, she found that the place had changed a lot in the four years she'd been away. "Miami had doubled in size, and that was just the beginning of the energy that would culminate [result] in the great Boom of 1922–1926." It seemed like everyone in America wanted to buy a place in the Florida sun. Thousands of real estate agents sold and resold pieces of Florida land. Even though much of this land was too watery to build houses on, land prices kept going up and up.

These were exciting times to be in Miami, and Douglas — now assistant editor at the *Herald* — lived at the center of the excitement. Douglas reported for the *Herald* and wrote for its editorial page. She also had a regular column of her own. "It was in the column that I started to talk about Florida as landscape and geography, to investigate it and to explore it," she said.

Douglas discovered that a small group of people were working hard to preserve the Everglades, southern Florida's unique wetlands. In her newspaper column she supported their efforts. Before long, in the early 1920s, she found herself put on the committee that was working to protect the area by establishing an Everglades National Park.

What is the Everglades, and why did Marjory Stoneman Douglas and her friends think it was so important to save it? The Everglades is an awfully uncomfortable place. It's covered with shallow water and thick, tall, sharp-edged sawgrass. Its wildlife includes poisonous snakes, alligators, and — especially — mosquitoes.

But the Everglades isn't just a nasty, buggy swamp. In fact, it isn't a swamp at all. It's a very wide, very shallow river — a "river of grass," in Douglas's words — that flows slowly south from

Water collects in shallow pools as it flows slowly through miles of grass in this photo of the Everglades.

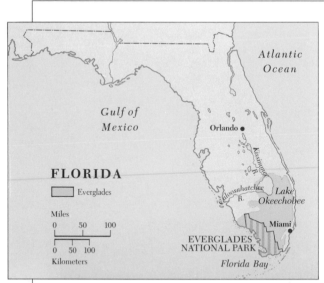

FLORIDA

☐ Everglades

Miles
0   50   100

0   50   100
Kilometers

Gulf of
Mexico

Atlantic
Ocean

Orlando ●

Kissimmee R.

Caloosahatchee R.

Lake
Okeechobee

Miami ●

EVERGLADES
NATIONAL PARK

Florida Bay

Left: As this map shows, only part of the Everglades is protected as a national park. Below: A manatee. The type of manatee found in the Everglades is known as the Caribbean Manatee.

Lake Okeechobee in central Florida down the middle of the state to empty into Florida Bay and the Gulf of Mexico.

This river of grass is home to many wild animals. Sharp-eyed ospreys glide over the Everglades, looking for fish to catch. Manatees — fishy-looking mammals larger than a full-grown person — swim in small groups in the Everglades' shallow waters. Deer, otters, opossums, rabbits and other rodents, turtles and toads, and many different kinds of fishes all live in the Everglades. The Everglades is a rich and diverse ecosystem — a community of plants and animals living together and depending on each other and on their surrounding environment for survival.

Some of the animals living in the Everglades ecosystem are rare and endangered species. Some cannot be found anywhere else. The Florida panther, for example, lives only in the southern part of Florida, and even there it is very rare indeed. It looks much like the kind of mountain lion that lives in the western half of the United States, and it was a great favorite of Marjory Stoneman Douglas. She described the only time she ever saw one face-to-face, early one morning when she was out for a walk:

A large, handsome panther emerged from the man-groves, moved slowly across the road and disappeared into the scrub brush on the other side. He wasn't twenty feet away. . . . I walked on and saw the tracks of his great, big fat furry footprints in the dust and sand of the road. Then it occurred to me that maybe the panther was looking at me, so I turned and scampered away. He decided not to follow.

They tell me that the panthers used to follow people, though they've never been known to hurt anybody.

¶he *Everglades* is the central fact of life in southern Florida. The river of grass provides fresh drinking water for all living things — including people. Without this fresh water, nothing could live there — no plants, no animals, and no people. Here's how it works:

The rock underneath southern Florida is

*The Everglades is also home to sleek panthers
like the one shown in this photo.*

shaped like a long spoon with a pointed end. This "spoon" holds the Everglades and all the dry land in southern Florida out of the surrounding salt water of the ocean. The bowl of the spoon is slightly tilted, so that its southern end is lower. Water flows over the spoon, very slowly, from Lake Okeechobee south through the Everglades — the river of grass. This water spills out over the tip of the spoon, at the southern end of Florida, into the sea.

This slow, steady flow of fresh water feeds the thousands of acres of sawgrass, and the many fish, birds, and other creatures of the Everglades. The water fills all the holes in the spongy-looking rock (limestone) that makes up the "spoon," and soaks the peat (plant remains) and muck that partly fill up the spoon. Wells tap into the fresh water collected in the holes in the rock to supply drinking water for Florida's towns and cities. And much of the water flowing over the Everglades evaporates in the hot Florida sun, creating the clouds that supply southern Florida's rainfall.

When the flowing fresh water reaches the end of the Everglades, it spills out into the Gulf of Mexico over the tip of the "spoon" and pushes back the sea's salt water. Without plenty of fresh water flowing over the Everglades, salt water would rush in to fill the bowl of the spoon. Salt water would kill the freshwater plants and animals — and it would poison the drinking-water wells.

Marjory Stoneman Douglas understood that both people and wildlife need the Everglades. She began pushing for government protection of the Everglades in the 1920s.

By then, the Everglades ecosystem already no longer worked as well as it ought to. For nearly a century, people had tried to drain water from parts of southern Florida. They wanted to turn wetland into land that people could run railroads over, and build on and farm. Fortunately, during this time so few people lived in southern Florida, and the job of controlling the water was so difficult, that most of the Everglades remained little changed.

Although the way the land looked didn't change much in these early years, people had a terrible effect on the region's wildlife. Most of southern Florida's huge numbers of beautiful wild birds — egrets, ibises, and herons — were killed so that their feathers could be used to decorate ladies' hats. And well into the 1900s, until very few were left alive, alligators were killed to provide leather for fancy shoes, belts, and wallets.

Still, the most serious changes people made to southern Florida's environment — changes in the water system — had barely begun when Marjory Stoneman Douglas first arrived in Miami. And much of the early drainage work — canals to take water away from wetlands, walls to keep water from flooding dry lands — was wiped out by a terrible hurricane in 1926.

Then, only two years later, another hurricane destroyed walls that had been built around Lake Okeechobee to keep floodwater away from houses and farms near the lake. Nearly two thousand people died in the flooding caused by this 1928 hurricane. Many more lost everything they owned.

People might have concluded from these catastrophes that they would just have to learn to live with nature's design for southern Florida — times of rain followed by times of dryness, or drought, with large areas left wet much of the time. Unfortu-

Right: This white ibis is one of the many birds that feeds off the small fish and frogs in the Everglades' waters—the same waters that this deadly alligator, below, patrols for prey.

Two hurricanes battered South Florida in 1926 and 1928. This photo shows boats tossed ashore and houses wrecked after the fierce 1926 storm.

nately for the Everglades, not many people thought this way.

Frank Stoneman, Marjory's father, was one of the few who did. Douglas remembered what happened when her father opposed the sugar planters and other farmers who wanted to drain land for farming just south of Lake Okeechobee:

My father wrote editorials against such drainage in 1906, and nearly went bankrupt as a result. People hated him for saying the Everglades shouldn't be drained. . . . Father was right and the governor and the rest of them were wrong.

Wrong or not, after the 1928 hurricane and flooding, a new wall was built around the southern end of Lake Okeechobee. This kept the lake from overflowing during seasons of heavy rain. Sugarcane and other field crops were planted south of the lake. A straight canal was dug from Lake Okeechobee to the Gulf of Mexico, replacing the slow, twisting-and-turning Caloosahatchee River. Whenever the water in the lake rose high enough to reach near the top of the new wall, enough water was rushed down the canal to keep the lake from over-flowing. The canal also supplied irrigation water for the farmland near the lake.

This flood-control project around Lake Okee-chobee did succeed in keeping many acres of land dry enough for farming. But it also cut off much of the water flowing to the Everglades.

Without a steady flow of fresh water south from Lake Okeechobee, the Everglades began to die. Dryland plants and animals began to crowd out the Everglades wildlife. Before the flood-control pro-ject, wildfires burned only in small areas at the driest time of the year. Now they burned out larger and larger patches of the Everglades. And, at the southern end of the state, there was no longer enough fresh water flowing from the Everglades to push back the sea's salt water. Foot by foot, salt water crept into southern Florida's wet places from the sea, killing plants and wildlife — and poisoning the drinking water.

While the heart of southern Florida — the Ever-glades — was slowly dying, cities and towns sprang

As more Everglades land was drained and dried out for development, more wildfires like the one shown here struck.

up along the state's east and west coasts. The state's population exploded as tens of thousands of people moved south to make their homes in the Florida sun. Miami — only a small frontier town when Marjory Stoneman Douglas moved there in the 1920s — became a big city.

These growing towns and cities needed more and more water. But, with less water flowing through the Everglades, and salt water creeping in from the ocean, fresh drinking water became harder to find. By the 1940s, salt water was working its way hundreds of feet farther inland each year.

Nineteen forty-four was a very dry year. So little rain fell, and the land became so dry, that fires burned not only the sawgrass but even the dried-out peaty soil of the Everglades. While most of the Everglades burned, salt water crept in from the coast faster than ever before. Finally, enough people understood that the way they treated water and land had to change — or southern Florida would become a place where no one could live.

Two kinds of change took place. First, the old dream of draining all of the Everglades died. People now knew enough about the river of grass to understand that much of it could never be made into useful farmland. And draining the Everglades endangered southern Florida's supply of fresh water.

Second, people came to agree that they needed one central authority to protect and manage all of southern Florida's water resources. After all, the area's water moves through one large ecosystem. Actions taken in one place can affect the water supply far away. In 1948, Florida created a special agency to handle all of southern and central Florida's water problems. The state also invited the U.S. Army Corps of Engineers to work with the new state agency to manage the water supply.

Along with these changes in attitudes toward and plans for the Everglades came a big change made by the federal government. In 1947 the Everglades National Park was finally established — a quarter century after Marjory Stoneman Douglas and other friends of the Everglades had first tried to convince the government that a park was needed. The new park made a large part of the original Everglades off-limits to farming and development. When President Harry S. Truman officially opened the park, Douglas watched the opening ceremony from a front-row seat.

That same year, 1947, Douglas published her great book about the Everglades, *The Everglades: River of Grass.* She hadn't planned to write such a book — it came about almost by accident.

A book publisher had asked her to write a book about the Miami River. Her reaction was: "You can't write a book about the Miami River. It's only about an inch long." She then asked if she could somehow use the Everglades to back up the Miami River and maybe get a book out of that. When the publisher agreed, Douglas said, "I was hooked with the idea that would consume me for the rest of my life."

It took Douglas five years to research and write *The Everglades: River of Grass.* It was a great success, and the many thousands of people who read it learned to appreciate the beauty of this unique and vitally important ecosystem and to understand how it worked.

Douglas spent the next twenty or so years writ-

Above: President Truman, at the left behind the podium, dedicates Everglades National Park. Douglas worked to establish the park for more than two decades. Right: After she achieved her goal, she moved on to writing books.

ing books. Some of her books were about Florida, and some were about other topics. One was about hurricanes. "I made the people of Charleston, South Carolina, furious by saying that their town had been hit by more hurricanes than any other town on the Atlantic seaboard," she recalled years later. "They said my pointing this out was bad for tourism and for real estate."

Through the 1950s and 1960s, Marjory Stoneman Douglas remained interested in the Everglades, but did not spend very much time working to preserve its health. There was not yet any real organized environmental movement working to "save" the Everglades ecosystem.

Unfortunately, the Everglades was still in danger. The state agency created in 1948 to manage the water supply turned out to be more of a friend to farmers and real estate developers than to the Everglades. Most of the Army Corps of Engineers' water-control projects were designed to make irrigation water available to farmers and dry land available to developers. As more and more land was planted with irrigated crops, and as more and more people moved to Florida's thirsty cities, less and less water was allowed to flow through the Everglades.

Many of the Everglades' problems have come from trouble upstream. Since much of the Everglades' water comes from the Kissimmee River, which feeds Lake Okeechobee, trouble for the Kissimmee means trouble for the Everglades. And the Kissimmee River has had terrible trouble indeed.

The Kissimmee used to be a slow, shallow, winding river. It took eleven days for water to run the length of the river, from Lake Kissimmee (near Orlando, well north of the Everglades) south to Lake Okeechobee. Water polluted by town sewers and farm chemicals oozed through the thousands of acres of wetlands near the river. These wetlands filtered out the pollution. The cleaned-up water then trickled slowly into Lake Okeechobee.

Then, in the early 1960s, the Army Corps of Engineers turned the curving Kissimmee River into an arrow-straight canal. Over the years, farmers and builders had plowed and built closer and closer to the river. They had begun to use land that

Top: The Kissimmee River twisted and turned on its
way to Lake Okeechobee, supplying water that helped
keep the Everglades healthy. Bottom: But when the
Army Corps of Engineers made the Kissimmee straight,
the Everglades suffered from pollution and drought.

the river sometimes flooded during rainy seasons. To stop the flooding, the Corps of Engineers dug a long, deep, straight ditch, turning the Kissimmee's 103 winding miles (166 kilometers) into a 56-mile (90-kilometer) canal. The wetlands along the old path of the Kissimmee River dried up. Water rushed down the new canal from Lake Kissimmee to Lake Okeechobee in only two days.

The canal did severe damage to the ecosystems farther south, including the Everglades. Instead of trickling in a slow, steady, even flow, water now poured down the canal in great gushes to Lake Okeechobee. Farmers and towns took most of this water. Only when the irrigation canals and town water-storage areas were full did the water over-flow from Lake Okeechobee into the Everglades. During the dry times between these great gushes of water, very little water reached the Everglades.

Worse still, the water was much more polluted, now that it no longer filtered through the Kissim-mee River's old wetlands. The Everglades and Lake Okeechobee's native plants and animals need a steady trickle of clean water. The dirty water poisoned some wildlife. And many plants and animals couldn't cope with the dramatic changes in the amount of water flowing through the ecosystem. When the Army Corps of Engineers opened the floodgates between Lake Okeechobee and the Everglades, the sudden rush of water sometimes washed away the nests of whole flocks of birds — along with all the baby birds in the nests.

During the 1960s, more and more people began to see how much trouble the Everglades was in. Then, around 1968, plans were made to build a huge jetport in the Everglades. The jetport project would have paved over an important part of the Everglades. News of these plans moved many people to action, to try to save the Everglades.

Marjory Stoneman Douglas had heard that Joe Browder, an acquaintance of hers, was working hard to stop the jetport. Here's her description of how, at the age of seventy-eight, she finally became a full-fledged environmental activist:

There was a gal working for Joe Browder by the name of Wilson. I met her one night in a grocery store and I said, "I think you and Joe are doing great work. It's wonderful." She looked me square

As the Everglades dried out, animals like this alligator found their habitats shrinking.

in the eye and said, "Yeah, what are you doing?"
"Oh me?" I said. "I wrote the book." "That's not
enough," she countered. We need people to help
us." To get out of this conversation, I casually
mumbled [something] like "I'll do whatever I can."

You couldn't say, "I'll do whatever I can" casu-
ally to Joe Browder. He was at my doorstep the next
day.

Douglas told Browder that she didn't think she
could do very much all by herself. She thought that
an organization would be more successful than any
individual could be in stopping the jetport.

Without skipping a beat, he said, "Well, why don't
you start an organization?" So there I was, stuck
with a challenge that began . . . in the grocery-store
line. . . . He took me out to visit the site of the
proposed jetport, right in the path of the flow of the
water across the wetlands. A small landing strip
for private planes had been put out there already,
and it had stopped some of the flow. He and I both
knew we didn't ever want to see a huge airport and
industrial park in the Everglades.

Douglas was all too well aware of the disastrous effects that lack of water had already had on the Everglades. She was still thinking about how to stop the jetport when she met an old friend one afternoon at a picnic.

I asked him what he thought about an organization that might be called something like the Friends of the Everglades — which anybody could join for, say, a dollar. Without hesitation he handed me a dollar. "I think it's a great idea."

Now I had not only the idea of an organization to contend with, but also one member and an endowment [money]. What choice did I have but to carry this further? . . . Soon, I started making speeches to every organization that would listen to me. . . . I got 15 or 20 new members, at $1 apiece, every time I spoke. . . .

The jetport was stopped — not necessarily through my efforts but through the efforts of many people. . . . The Friends of the Everglades was continued, and soon we turned our attentions from the single jetport project to the general predicament of the water.

Marjory Stoneman Douglas speaking on behalf of Friends of the Everglades.

Through the 1970s and 1980s and into the 1990s, Marjory Stoneman Douglas and Friends of the Everglades tackled many environmental problems. They always had one goal in mind: to keep plenty of clean, fresh water flowing freely through the river of grass.

Marjory's Army (as Friends of the Everglades sometimes calls itself) worked hard to close drainage canals. They fought for stronger restrictions on farming and building activities that might hurt the Everglades. And they worked to preserve the habitat of endangered species living in the Everglades.

To be a friend of the Everglades, Douglas was never afraid to take on powerful enemies. "We're fighting the federal government, the U.S. Army Corps of Engineers, water management, [and] realtors," she once said.

Douglas understood how Kissimmee, Okeechobee, and the Everglades are all connected and dependent on each other. She saw that it's not possible to keep the Everglades healthy without also taking care of the water farther north. "It's the whole thing that's got to be preserved," Douglas said. "We've got to restore the Kissimmee River, we've got to clean up Lake Okeechobee and maintain the . . . flow of the Everglades."

Friends of the Everglades and other environmental groups for years made the Kissimmee River a top priority. Their dedication paid off. In 1992 the Army Corps of Engineers finally began restoring the Kissimmee River, allowing it once again to flow through many of its old twists and turns.

But the river, like the Everglades, will never again be exactly like it was a hundred years ago. Too many changes have already been made, and too many people now live close enough to these ecosystems to allow the natural cycles of flood and fire to occur without human interference.

The Everglades today has shrunk to half its original size. Although the Everglades hasn't died, it is constantly threatened by the effects of so many people living so close by. The Everglades will always need the watchful protection of friends like Marjory Stoneman Douglas.

Fortunately, most people in Florida now understand — as they didn't fifty years ago — that the Everglades must be preserved, and not only because they are uniquely beautiful and naturally teeming with wildlife. The Everglades' water system is also essential to *human* life in Florida. Marjory Stoneman Douglas, by writing and speaking about the subject for so many years, convinced more people of this truth than did anyone else.

O*ver her long life,* Douglas had three successful careers. First, she wrote newspaper and magazine articles. Next, beginning with *River of Grass,* she wrote books. Finally, while still continuing to write, she became a full-time environmentalist.

When Marjory Stoneman Douglas began her third career by founding Friends of the Everglades, she was already seventy-eight years old. Not only was she well past the age at which most people retire — she was also going blind, from an inherited eye problem.

Even so, she never felt she was too old or too frail to keep speaking out for the environment. For another quarter century she spoke about the Everglades to just about any group that was willing to listen. Recognized wherever she went, in her lady-

Marjory Stoneman Douglas and President Bill Clinton at the ceremony during which she received the Medal of Freedom.

like flowered dresses, panama straw hat, and single string of white beads, Marjory Stoneman Douglas became a much-loved public figure. Even after her hundredth birthday, on April 7, 1990, she continued to make speeches about and lend her support to keeping the Everglades healthy.

In 1993, President Bill Clinton invited 103-year-old Marjory Stoneman Douglas to Washington, DC. On November 30, at the White House, the president presented Douglas with the Medal of Freedom, the highest presidential honor given to civilians in the United States. President Clinton called Douglas the "grandmother of the Glades." Tiny, frail Douglas stood up from a wheelchair to accept the award. Then she saluted the audience, waving her hand. Her friends said she couldn't have been happier.

Important Dates

━━━━━━━━

1890	Born April 7 in Minneapolis, Minnesota. She and her family soon move to Taunton, Massachusetts, where Marjory attends elementary school and high school.
1912	Earns bachelor's degree from Wellesley.
1915	Moves to Miami, Florida, and goes to work writing for the Miami *Herald.*
1917	Enlists in the Naval Reserve. Is sent by the Red Cross to Europe.
1920s	Serves on a committee working to establish a national park in the Everglades.
1926	Builds a small house in Coconut Grove.
1920s–40s	Writes newspaper and magazine articles, sometimes about life in southern Florida.
1947	*The Everglades: River of Grass* is published. Everglades National Park opens.
1940s–60s	Writes books about nature and history.
1969	Organizes Friends of the Everglades to protect and restore the Everglades ecosystem.
1970s–90s	Continues to write, but now spends most of her time working to save the Everglades.
1993	Receives the Medal of Freedom.

Further Reading

By Marjory Stoneman Douglas

The Everglades: River of Grass. St. Simons Island, GA: Mockingbird Books, 1974.

(with John Rothchild) *Voice of the River.* Sarasota, FL: Pineapple Press, 1987.

About Marjory Stoneman Douglas

Bryant, Jennifer. *Marjory Stoneman Douglas: Voice of the Everglades.* New York: Twenty-First Century Books, 1992.

About the Everglades

Linn, Christopher. *Everglades: Exploring the Unknown.* Mahwah, NJ: Troll Associates, 1976.

Morgan, Cheryl K. *The Everglades.* Mahwah, NJ: Troll Associates, 1990.

Radlauer, Ruth. *Everglades National Park.* Chicago: Childrens Press, 1976.

Sources

Most of the information in this book is derived from Marjory Stoneman Douglas's memoirs, *Voice of the River* (Pineapple Press, 1987); from her *The Everglades: River of Grass* (Mockingbird Books, 1974); from the many newspaper and magazine articles written about Douglas; and from various works on natural history that include material about southern Florida but not necessarily about Douglas herself.

All of the quotes are from *Voice of the River,* except for these few:

p. 5: "It's got to be done . . ." is from the Miami *Herald*'s coverage of Marjory Stoneman Douglas's April 1990 Earth Day speech.

p. 39: "We're fighting . . ." is from *Time*'s January 31, 1983, article about Douglas.

p. 39: "It's the whole thing . . ." is from *Audubon* magazine's lengthy 1991 profile of Douglas.

Index